# WHY CAN'T
# I DO
# WHATEVER I WANT?

*Designed for pressure. Shaped by Christ.*

By D.A. Cook

Published by Bring Back the Fire Publishing

ISBN: ISBN: 978-0-9851820-3-8

Printed in the United States of America

*"And the LORD God commanded the man, saying, 'You may surely eat of every tree of the garden, but of the tree of the knowledge of good and evil you shall not eat, for in the day that you eat of it you shall surely die.'"*

— *Genesis 2:16–17 (ESV)*

# THE PATTERN I COULD NOT IGNORE

If you have ever felt stuck while watching other people move forward, this is for you. If you have ever wondered why you can finish some things effortlessly but cannot seem to start others, no matter how much they matter, you are not alone.
 If you have ever been told you just need more discipline, more focus, more motivation, and none of that advice ever actually worked, I understand. I have been there. I lived there for years.

This is not a book written from the outside looking in. This is written from someone who could not figure out why they kept stalling, kept drifting, kept failing to finish the things that mattered most. Until I finally saw the pattern.

I spent most of my adult life frustrated—not because I never finished anything, but because I couldn't finish what mattered most to me: my personal goals, ideas, and the work I wanted to be known for. That gap nearly broke me.

I tried everything people said should work. I watched the videos. I read the books. I built systems. I cleaned my desk. I cleaned my house. I used timers. I blocked time. I followed routines. I chased discipline. None of it worked.

I did not give up, and that was part of the pain. I kept trying, which somehow made it worse. I was not lazy. I was not short on ideas. Ideas were never my problem. I had more ideas than I could hold. What I had was a growing fear I could not shake.

I remember lying in bed thinking that I was going to die with nothing done that actually mattered to me. Not the responsibilities I fulfilled. Not the things I had to do. But the things I said were important to me. The things I believed I was meant to build. That thought sat heavy in my chest.

I would wake up with ideas every day. New ones. Clear ones. Good ones. Brands. Books. Projects. Directions. And yet I could not move. I would open my laptop, stare at the screen, and close it again. Not because I did not know what to do, but because nothing in me would engage.

I watched a lot of Netflix. Not because I was resting, but because it was easier than choosing. Episodes ended. Nothing else did.

What confused me most was the contradiction in my own life. When I look back honestly, I finished things very well under certain conditions. In the military, I completed creative work on impossible timelines. Videos due in twenty-four hours. Scripts, narration, editing, and delivery. I learned to work in five-minute windows because I had no choice. The work had to be done. People were waiting. Standards existed. And I did good work. I got better and better at it.

When I signed up for races, I trained. When I had a fitness test scheduled, I worked out. When passing mattered, I passed.

Once, without fully realizing why, I parked my car two miles away from my house so I would have to jog home and jog back in the morning. I created pressure without understanding it.

As a parent, I showed up. My daughters needed me, and that was not negotiable. You do not get to opt out when someone depends on you. When your kids need you present, you show up. I did not always understand why I could be so consistent there and so scattered everywhere else, but I was. Being their mom mattered more than my own confusion.

Years earlier, when I ran a live morning show, I showed up every day because people were waiting for me. If I did not show up, I would let them down.

That was the pattern. Every time I finished something, there was a constraint. Every time I drifted, there was open space. I did not arrive at that realization casually. I dug into myself every way I knew how. I watched hours of videos trying to understand why I could not follow through. I read about productivity, discipline, focus, and motivation. I asked for advice. I went to counseling. I tried every tool and resource I could find, searching for something that would finally make my behavior make sense.

Then, in a conversation I had with a friend, a simple question cut through. She asked me, when I finish something, what actually makes me finish?

The answer was uncomfortable. It was not motivation. It was not inspiration. It was not clarity. It was boundaries. Deadlines. Consequences. Limits I could not negotiate with.

At the same time, I noticed something else. When those limits were absent, my body shut down. I did not feel energized. I did not feel free. I did not feel motivated. I felt heavy. Still. Unresponsive. I stayed in bed longer. I avoided starting. I avoided choosing.

This was not defiance. It was not apathy. Nothing anyone told me explained that.

It was my nervous system.

No one had ever explained that to me. I was not failing because I needed better habits. I was not failing because I needed more discipline. I was not failing because I needed the right system. I was failing because my nervous system did not mobilize without constraint. When nothing was required, nothing moved.

That realization reframed my entire life. I was not broken. I was uncontained. That changed everything. Because if the problem wasn't me, if the problem was missing constraints, then I could finally stop fighting myself and start recognizing what my body actually needed to move.

# MOTIVATION WAS NOT THE PROBLEM

For a long time, I believed what I had been told. If I could not act, it meant I did not want it badly enough. If I could not follow through, it meant I lacked discipline. If I could not stay consistent, it meant something was wrong with my mindset. So I tried to fix myself.

I studied motivation. I studied dopamine. I studied habits, discipline, focus, reward systems, ADHD, productivity science, personality tests, and behavior hacks. I kept assuming the problem lived in my thinking. If I could just find the right explanation, the right insight, or the right method, something would finally click.

Nothing did.

I kept circling. Ideas everywhere. Books I wanted to write. Podcasts I wanted to make. Messages I felt called to share. I would get angry when I saw things in the world I wanted to respond to. My message mattered. I knew it did. But I could not get it out.

I thought maybe it was hormones. Menopause. Depression. But I was so tired of starting and believing and spending entire days inside an idea and never following through. What was wrong with me?
I pulled up videos about anxiety. Breathwork. Dopamine resets. I started practicing things I learned. Watching more.

And buried in the messaging was something I had heard before but never really paid attention to. The nervous system response.

It was not buried. It was plain as day. I just had not been looking for it.

If the nervous system was responsible for my anxiety, and I could regulate it, was my nervous system also keeping me from doing things?

People talk about the nervous system and anxiety all the time. Fight or flight. Resets. Regulation. But no one was connecting it to finishing things. My biggest problem. They talked about calming down. Not about why I could not start.

Could I really create conditions to cause my body to fight with my ideas? To get me to follow through?

I did the research. And here is what I found.

The nervous system is not concerned with goals, dreams, or long-term plans. It is concerned with survival, safety, and stability. It is constantly asking one question, often before we are even aware of it. Is action required right now?

Not, is this meaningful? Not, will this matter later? Not, do I feel inspired?

But, **is action required now**?

When the answer is yes, the body mobilizes. Energy appears. Focus sharpens. Action follows. When the answer is no, the body conserves energy. It slows down. It stays still.

That stillness often gets labeled as procrastination, avoidance, fatigue, depression, or anxiety, especially in wide open space. But it is not a moral failure. It is a biological response.

This explained everything. This explained everything. Why can I perform only under deadlines? Why could I finish what others depended on but not what I cared about alone? Why motivation talks made me anxious instead of productive. Why silence and space did not heal me, but paralyzed me.

My nervous system did not need encouragement. It needed the right conditions.

Motivation can create a temporary surge of energy, but energy without structure does not produce action. It produces tension. That is why so many people feel briefly inspired, only to crash harder than before. Motivation stimulates. The nervous system stabilizes.

This realization quietly dissolved a layer of shame I had been carrying for years. If the nervous system does not perceive urgency, safety, or consequence, it will not mobilize. No amount of wanting can override that. No amount of self-criticism can fix it. I was not broken. I was responding to my environment.

Understanding this did not make me passive. It made me accurate. It shifted the question from what is wrong with me to what does my nervous system recognize as a signal to move.

That shift changed everything. Because once you understand this is about design, not deficiency, you stop asking motivation to do biology's job. You can finally start working with yourself instead of against yourself.

# DESIGN WITH PURPOSE

I am a Christian. So, when I realized my nervous system needed constraints to move, I got excited and started looking for this in Scripture. And it is actually there.

God designed this.

The thing I thought was an obstacle was actually a constraint. The kind of constraint I needed. And it was not blocking me. It was making it possible.

That shift changed everything. Because for most of my life, I treated limits as problems. Deployment coming up. Certifications I had to finish. Responsibilities piling on when all I wanted was to write my books and build my ideas. Every constraint felt like an obstacle. Like if I could just get past this one thing, then I could finally do what mattered.

But the constraint was not the problem. My fight against it was.

When I saw the limit as an obstacle, my nervous system froze. When I saw it as the mechanism, my nervous system engaged. The constraint was the same. My relationship to it changed everything.

Once I stopped resisting and started looking, the pattern was everywhere in Scripture.

Genesis 1. God does not create in chaos. He creates through separation. Light from darkness. Waters above from waters below. Sea from dry land. Day from night. Creation itself is an act of boundary making. Things are defined by what they are not. Constraint creates form.

Then the rhythm. Evening, morning. Day one. Day two. Time as constraint. God does not work in timelessness. He works in days. Six days of work, one day of rest. The rhythm itself is a limit.

And Genesis 2 verse 2 through 3. God rests. Not because He is tired. Because the work is finished. Rest is not the absence of constraint. It is the ultimate constraint. Stop. The boundary of completion. Without it, work never ends. It just drifts.

Before anything went wrong, before shame, before fear, before sin entered the story, there was already a boundary. That detail matters. Eden is often treated as a morality tale, but the order of events tells a deeper truth. The boundary did not appear after failure. It was present from the beginning.
God places Adam and Eve in a garden described as good, abundant, and lacking nothing. Freedom is not scarce in Eden. It is expansive. They are given access, responsibility, and relationship. And within that freedom, there is a single boundary. One tree. One no.

If limits only exist because humans are untrustworthy, then they would not appear in a world God calls very good. But the boundary is there before anything is broken. Which means the limit was not punishment. It was part of the design. The tree itself is not described as evil. The command is not framed as cruelty. The boundary simply marks a distinction. God is God. Humans are not. Reality is received, not defined. When I saw that, everything clicked. What looked like obstacles were actually constraints. Intentional ones.

Psalm 16 verse 5 through 6. David writes, "The LORD is my chosen portion and my cup; you hold my lot. The lines have fallen for me in pleasant places; indeed, I have a beautiful inheritance."

Most people skip over that word. Lines. It sounds poetic. Metaphorical. Safe.

It is not.

The Hebrew word is chavalim. Measuring cords. The ropes they used to mark off land boundaries. Literal constraints. David is not talking about abstract blessings. He is talking about the limits God gave him.

And he calls them pleasant. Not tolerable. Not necessary. Pleasant.

He is thanking God for boundaries. For the measured portion. For the inheritance that only exists because lines were drawn around it. Without the lines, there is no inheritance. Without the constraint, there is nothing to hold.

David is not waiting for freedom from limits. He is recognizing that the limits themselves are the gift.

That became my prayer. The thing I thought was an obstacle was actually a constraint I needed. My resistance to it was the problem. The constraint was the gift. I just had to stop fighting it.

Moses. Called to lead but shaped by obscurity. By weakness. By a desert that narrowed his options. Even when he is sent, he is still bound by dependence. He does not speak well. He does not move independently. God does not remove these limits to prove His power. He works through them.

The Ten Commandments. Not arbitrary rules meant to restrict life. They function as load bearing boundaries. They govern time, desire, truth, rest, relationship, and responsibility.

Thou shalt not steal. Without that boundary, trust collapses. Commerce stops. Community unravels. Property means nothing. The constraint is not oppression. It is what holds society together.

Thou shalt not murder. Without that limit, life has no value. Safety disappears. Fear governs everything. The boundary is not restrictive. It is what allows people to exist near each other without constant threat.

Remember the Sabbath. Without that constraint, work never stops. Rest becomes impossible. The body breaks down. The rhythm of one day in seven is not a burden. It is what keeps you from dissolving into endless motion.

These are not punishments. They are structure. Without them, things do not become freer. They fall apart.

Paul. Imprisonment, opposition, physical limitation. None of these remove his calling. They concentrate it. His most enduring work is written within confinement. Constraint does not silence him. It gives his words weight.

Jesus. He enters the world through incarnation, not dominance. He submits to time, place, obedience, and the will of the Father. He lives within boundaries He does not create. That submission is not weakness. It is the means through which life is restored.

God does not reveal Himself as a remover of limits, but as their author. He sets boundaries because without them, creation fractures. Freedom without form does not produce life. It produces collapse.

The limits in my life were not obstacles. They were load bearing constraints. My job was not to move the boulder. It was to accept it. To stop fighting it. To recognize that the constraint was not blocking my calling. It was the very thing making it possible.

# WHEN THE CONSTRAINTS FELT LIKE THREATS

Deployment was coming. Certifications were due. I had just started a SaaS business. Built software. Poured everything into it. And now I had to leave it.

Responsibilities were piling on. Every new requirement felt like it was suffocating me. I could not breathe. The walls were closing in.

This was not the plan. I had ideas. Books I wanted to write. I wanted to build a business. A message I needed to get out. And everything I cared about felt blocked by something I had not chosen.

The constraints felt like threats, not tools.

My body responded the way it was designed to. Fight or flight. I felt so much pressure. What I know now was my nervous system locking into high gear. I was not resisting out of rebellion. I was frozen. Overwhelmed. Stuck.

I had been working on my anxiety for months. Deep breathing. Vagus nerve regulation. All the tools. And it was working. The anxiety was getting better.

But I felt sad. Dull. Life sucked.

Because I had all these things I had to do. And all these things I wanted to do. And I thought the things I had to do were blocking the things I wanted to do.

I was stuck between obligation and desire. Between deployment prep and books I wanted to write. Between certifications and the message I wanted to get out.

I kept waiting for the field to clear. For the responsibilities to be done. For the space to open up so I could finally do what mattered.

I was fighting to get out. And then I realized something. I am a person who thinks quickly. Ideas come and go. What if I stop waiting and just write the book? In the middle of everything else. I can write it in two days. I can finish the deployment prep. I can knock out the certifications.

I did not need to clear the field. I needed to stop treating them as separate.

So I wrote. Not when I had time. Not when the pressure lifted. Under the pressure. In the middle of deployment prep. In the gaps between certifications. In the tight windows I thought were too small to matter.

I finished a book in two days. Why You Can't Hear God. Not because I suddenly had time. Because I stopped waiting for the constraints to disappear.

I was able to relax. And do the work. And enjoy it. On all fronts.

I was not sad anymore. I could get out of bed. Life had meaning again.

I stopped fighting myself. I stopped fighting the constraints in my life. I welcomed them. As a friend. Something that would help me and push me to finish things.

And that is how I actually function. Quick thinking. Tight windows. Real deadlines. Pressure.

The deployment was not blocking me. It was creating the exact conditions I needed to move. The certifications were not delaying my work. They were the pressure that made me actually do it. The responsibilities piling up were not obstacles. They were the design.

I hired people to help with my house. I finished the things I had to do. I wrote the things I wanted to write. Not one after the other. At the same time.

The constraints were not the enemy. Waiting for them to disappear was.

When I stopped fighting and started working with the pressure, everything changed. I did not need the field cleared.

I needed the constraints in place. That is how I work best. Under pressure. In tight windows. With real stakes.

And when I finally realized that, I did not just finish a book. I published it. I had a lot of half-written books. But this time I actually published. Stayed up late to finish it. And then went right into my certifications and deployment prep.

The obstacles were never obstacles. They were the very things making it possible.

.

# RECOGNIZING YOUR DESIGN

Here is what many people miss.

We are all different. Not slightly different. Wildly, intentionally, creatively different. God did not make copies. He made originals.

That is why what works for one person fails completely for another. That is why advice can sound perfect and do nothing. That is why you can read a book, follow the steps, and still feel stuck.

You are not doing it wrong. You are just not them.

God made us to respond differently. To move differently. To worship differently. To work differently. Some people come alive in silence. Others need noise. Some people thrive in routine. Others suffocate in it. Some need pressure. Others need space.

This is not a flaw in creation. This is the point of creation. And the same is true with constraints.

What constrains you might liberate someone else. What helps you might crush them. The constraint that makes you freeze might be exactly what makes someone else move.

This is where most people get lost. They see someone thriving under a certain kind of pressure and think, "I should be able to do that too." So they try. And they fail. And they assume something is wrong with them.

Nothing is wrong with you. You just need different constraints.

If you want to understand how you are designed, you have to stop copying and start observing.

Look at the last few things you actually finished. Not the things you started. Not the things you meant to do. The things you completed.

What was present?

Was there a deadline? A real one. Time running out. Pressure building. Did that wake you up? Or did it shut you down? Was someone counting on you? A person waiting. A responsibility you could not walk away from. Did that move you? Or did it weigh you down?

Was there a clear structure? A plan. A system. Steps you could follow. Did that help you engage? Or did it feel like a cage? Were there real stakes? Consequences if you did not act. Something on the line. Did that focus you? Or did it paralyze you?

The pattern is information. It is telling you how you are wired. It is showing you what your nervous system recognizes as a signal to move.

Some people only finish when time is tight. Deadlines sharpen their focus. Urgency clears the fog. When a clock is ticking, their body wakes up and organizes itself. Without a clear end date, they drift. Open timelines feel generous, but nothing ever quite starts.

Others do not respond to time at all. They can stare at a deadline and feel nothing. But the moment someone else is depending on them, everything changes. Responsibility flips a switch. Showing up for another person gives their energy direction. They are not lazy when left alone. They are relationally activated.

Some people need structure before they can act. They do not move well in chaos or open space. They need clear lanes, predictable rhythms, and defined containers. This is often misunderstood as rigidity, but it is actually regulation. Structure tells their nervous system it is safe enough to engage. Without it, they feel overwhelmed before they ever begin.

Others resist structure entirely. Routines feel suffocating. Schedules drain their energy instead of organizing it. What helps them is consequence. Stakes. A real cost if they do not act. When something is on the line, they move. When nothing matters immediately, they stall. It is not that they do not care. It is that their system does not respond until the outcome is tangible.

You are one of these. Maybe a combination. But you are not all of them. And trying to be will break you.

This is why comparing yourself to others is so damaging. You see someone thriving under conditions that quietly undo you and assume you are deficient. You are not. You are differently designed.

Now here is the part that changes everything.

The constraints you are fighting right now might be the ones you need.

Go back to what feels like an obstacle in your life. The thing you keep trying to get past. The responsibility you wish would disappear. The deadline you resent. The structure you are trying to escape.

What if it is not blocking you? What if it is revealing how you are designed?

I fought deployment. I fought certifications. I fought every responsibility that piled on when all I wanted was space to write. I thought if I could just clear the field, I could finally do what mattered.

But the field being full was not the problem. My resistance to it was.

Once I stopped fighting and started paying attention, I realized something. I do not work well with lots of time. I work best under pressure. In tight windows. With real stakes. That is not a flaw. That is my design.

The constraint I was fighting was the exact condition I needed to move.

You might be doing the same thing. Resisting the very thing that would help you function.

You cannot force yourself into someone else's pattern. Their rhythm is not yours. Their constraints are not yours. What mobilizes them might paralyze you. What helps them might hurt you.

Stop trying to copy. Start paying attention.

When do you actually move? When do you finish? When does your body engage instead of shut down?

That is your design revealing itself.

And once you see it, you stop asking what is wrong with you. You start asking what kind of constraint actually brings you to life.

That question is not self-indulgent. It is responsible. Because if limits are unavoidable, then learning which ones form you instead of flatten you matters.

You are not broken for being different. You are designed.

# CONSTRAINTS SHOW UP FOR YOU

Here is what I tried first. I tried to create my own constraints. I set deadlines for myself. I built accountability systems. I told people what I was going to do so I would feel pressure to follow through. I made lists. I blocked time. I created structure.

None of it worked.

Because my nervous system knew the difference. Manufactured pressure is not real pressure. A deadline you invented is not the same as a deadline someone else set. Accountability you engineered is not the same as responsibility that lands on you whether you want it or not. You cannot fake a constraint. Your body knows.

Sometimes you do create your own constraints. But they only work if they are real. If you give yourself no other choice.
I once got on a ski lift without knowing how to ski. I went to the top of the mountain to force myself to ski down. That was a constraint. I had no choice. I could not undo it. I was at the top. The only way down was to ski.

I was terrible. I fell. I was scared. My boyfriend at the time had to literally help me down. But I got down. Not because I was ready. Because I had no other option.

That constraint worked. Not because I convinced myself it mattered. But because it was real. I had removed every other option.

But most of the time, we cannot do that. We cannot force ourselves into situations where there is no escape. And even when we can, it does not always produce what we need. Proverbs 16 verse 9. "The heart of man plans his way, but the LORD establishes his steps."

We make plans. We try to set things up. But God is the one who establishes the steps. He is the one who brings the constraints that actually move us. Not the ones we engineer. The ones He places.

I spent years trying to engineer the conditions I needed. And I kept failing. Not because I was doing it wrong. But because I was trying to do something that was never mine to do. Constraints do not come from you. They come to you.

Deployment was not something I manufactured. Certifications were not something I chose. Responsibilities piling on were not part of my plan. They showed up. And I resented them. Because I thought they were blocking me.

But they were not random. They were not accidents. And they were not obstacles. They were designed. For me. By God.

Once I saw that, everything shifted. I stopped trying to create constraints and started recognizing the ones already in my life. The ones I had been fighting. The ones I thought were in my way.

God brings the constraints you need. Not the ones you want. Not the ones that feel comfortable. The ones that actually move you.

Matthew 11 verse 28 through 30. Jesus says, "Come to me, all who labor and are heavy laden, and I will give you rest. Take my yoke upon you, and learn from me, for I am gentle and lowly in heart, and you will find rest for your souls. For my yoke is easy, and my burden is light."

He does not say, "I will remove the yoke." He says, "Take mine."

The constraint is not the problem. The wrong constraint is. The yoke you are trying to carry on your own is crushing you. His yoke fits. His yoke is designed for you
.

That is what I had been missing. I was trying to build my own yoke. My own pressure. My own constraints. And they were suffocating me because they were not from Him.

Romans 8 verse 28. "And we know that for those who love God all things work together for good, for those who are called according to his purpose."

All things. Not just the things you choose. Not just the things that feel good. All things. Including the constraints you did not ask for. Including the pressure you resent. Including the responsibilities you wish would disappear.

God is working through them. Not in spite of them
.

The deployment was not in my way. It was working together for good. The certifications were not delaying my calling. They were part of it. The constraints were not blocking me. They were forming me.

James 1 verse 2 through 4. "Count it all joy, my brothers, when you meet trials of various kinds, for you know that the testing of your faith produces steadfastness. And let steadfastness have its full effect, that you may be perfect and complete, lacking in nothing."

Trials. Testing. Not comfort. Not ease. Not open space.
The constraint is the test. And the test produces steadfastness. Completeness. Maturity.

You do not become complete by avoiding pressure. You become complete by moving through it.

This is what Christians do. We recognize constraints and we submit to them. Not because we are weak. But because we trust the One who placed them.

Following Christ is not about engineering your own life. It is about accepting what is set before you. It is about taking the yoke He gives, not the one you make.

And here is what I discovered. You become an overcomer not by resisting constraints, but by welcoming them.

1 John 5 verse 4 through 5. "For everyone who has been born of God overcomes the world. And this is the victory that has overcome the world, our faith. Who is it that overcomes the world except the one who believes that Jesus is the Son of God?"

Overcomer. That word gets thrown around a lot in Christian circles. But look at what it actually says. The victory is faith. Not effort. Not escape. Not getting out of the hard thing. Faith. Believing. Trusting that the constraint in front of you is not the enemy.

I used to think overcoming meant getting past the obstacle. Pushing through it. Defeating it. Moving on to something better.

But overcoming is not about escaping the constraint. It is about moving through it with Christ. It is about recognizing that the pressure is not crushing you. It is forming you.

The deployment was not something to overcome by avoiding it. It was something to move through. The certifications were not something to defeat. They were something to finish. The constraints were not enemies. They were conditions.

And when I stopped resisting them and started welcoming them, I did not just survive. I thrived.

I wrote. I finished. I published. I moved. Not because the pressure disappeared. But because I stopped fighting it.

Constraints come to you. You do not manufacture them. You do not engineer them. You recognize them. You submit to them. You welcome them as the very thing God is using to move you.

That is what it means to follow Him. That is what it means to take His yoke. That is what it means to overcome.

# BE ANXIOUS FOR NOTHING

Philippians 4 verse 6 through 7 changed my life. Not just spiritually. Biologically. All of me.

"Do not be anxious about anything, but in everything by prayer and supplication with thanksgiving let your requests be made known to God. And the peace of God, which surpasses all understanding, will guard your hearts and your minds in Christ Jesus."

This is the word of God. Not good advice. Not helpful tips. The word of God.

I had read that verse a thousand times. I had heard it preached. I had memorized it as a kid. But I did not live it until I had to.

When deployment was coming and certifications were piling on and responsibilities felt like they were suffocating me, I went back to this verse. Not as a nice idea. As a lifeline.
If Jesus says do not be anxious, then I have to believe that. I have to trust that. Because if I cannot trust Him with this, I cannot trust Him with anything.

So I made it more than something I read. I made it something I sang. I threw myself into it.

I used AI to create a song from Philippians 4 verse 6 through 7. I listened to it over and over. I sang it until I had it memorized. Not the tune. The truth. The words became part of me.

This took practice. This was not something I read once and moved on. Every time I was nervous, I practiced putting this in my mind. I sang it. I spoke it. I lived it.

Do not be anxious about anything. Not some things. **Anything.**

Look at how it is written. <u>Be anxious</u>. <u>For nothing</u>.

It starts with the anxiousness. God does not pretend it is not there. He names it. Be anxious. And then He negates it. For nothing.

That is not a suggestion. That is a command. And it is not cruel. It is care.

God does not tell you not to be anxious and then leave you on your own to figure it out. He tells you how. Prayer. Supplication. Thanksgiving. Let your requests be made known to God.

# WHY IT WORKS: MIND, BODY, SOUL

This is not abstract. This is real. Mind, body, soul, heart, spirit. All of you.

Deuteronomy 6 verse 5. "You shall love the LORD your God with all your heart and with all your soul and with all your might."

All your heart. All your soul. All your might. Not just one part of you. All of you.

When you bring God's word into your mind, it does not just sit there as information. It changes you. Your mind. Your body. Your soul. Your heart. Your spirit.

Psalm 19 verse 14. "Let the words of my mouth and the meditation of my heart be acceptable in your sight, O LORD, my rock and my redeemer."

Words of your mouth. Meditation of your heart. Both. Spoken and internal. Vocalized and believed.

Psalm 1 verse 2. "His delight is in the law of the LORD, and on his law he meditates day and night."

Day and night. Not once. Not when it is convenient. Constantly. Meditating. Repeating. Living in it.

Proverbs 4 verse 20 through 22. "My son, be attentive to my words; incline your ear to my sayings. Let them not escape from your sight; keep them within your heart. For they are life to those who find them, and healing to all their flesh." Life. Healing. To all your flesh. Not just your soul. Your body. Your flesh. God's word heals all of you.

This is not new age. This is not meditation techniques borrowed from somewhere else. God said it first. God owns it. Because He made you. He knows how you work. He designed your mind, your body, your soul to respond to His word.

When you pray, you vocalize. You breathe. You surrender control. Your nervous system recognizes safety. The act of speaking to God, of bringing your anxiety to Him, regulates you. Not just spiritually. Physically.

Repetition rewires your brain. When you repeat something, especially vocally, especially with emotion, especially with rhythm like music, you are creating and strengthening neural pathways. This is called neuroplasticity. Your brain physically changes.

But it is more than neurons. It is your spirit responding to God's spirit. It is your soul aligning with truth. It is your body recognizing the word of the One who made it.

Vocalization engages the vagus nerve. Singing. Humming. Chanting. These all stimulate the vagus nerve, which is the main nerve of your parasympathetic nervous system. That is your rest and digest system. It literally calms your body down. Lowers your heart rate. Regulates your breathing. Brings you out of fight or flight.

God designed that. He made your body to respond to vocalization. To sound. To singing. To speaking His word out loud.

David knew this. Psalm 55 verse 17. "Evening and morning and at noon I utter my complaint and moan, and he hears my voice."

He did not pray silently. He uttered. He moaned. He vocalized his anxiety. And God heard him.

Music and memory go deeper. When you put words to music, your brain encodes them differently. It is not just semantic memory, facts you know. It is episodic and emotional memory. That is why you can remember song lyrics from twenty years ago but forget what you read yesterday.

Words become belief through repetition. Your brain does not distinguish between I am telling myself this and this is true when you repeat it enough. Especially when you add emotion. Singing with feeling. Vocalizing out loud. The repetition literally changes what your nervous system believes is true.

But it is not just biology. It is the word of God entering you. Changing you. Healing you. Guarding you.

I needed that. When the pressure felt like too much, I sang. When the constraints felt like they were choking me, I vocalized the truth. Do not be anxious about anything.
And something happened that I did not expect. Peace.
Not the absence of pressure. Not the removal of constraints.
Peace in the middle of them.

"And the peace of God, which surpasses all understanding, will guard your hearts and your minds in Christ Jesus."
That word. Guard. The Greek word is phroureo. It means to protect by a military guard. To keep watch. To garrison.
The peace of God does not just comfort you. It guards you. It protects your heart. It protects your mind. It stands watch over you when everything else feels like it is falling apart.
This is not fluffy. This is real.

When I sang that verse, when I prayed it, when I brought my anxiety to God with thanksgiving, my body responded. My soul responded. My spirit responded. The crushing weight lifted. Not because the deployment went away. Not because the certifications disappeared. But because I was no longer carrying them alone.

The constraint was still there. But the anxiety was not. That is what this verse does. It does not remove the pressure. It guards you in the middle of it.

I could work. I could write. I could finish things. Not because I had figured out how to manage my anxiety on my own. But because I had given it to God. And He gave me peace that made no sense.

That is what surpasses all understanding means. It does not make sense. The pressure is real. The deadlines are real. The responsibilities are real. And yet you are at peace. That is not natural. That is supernatural.

The science confirms what God already knew. He designed your body to respond to His word. Mind, body, soul, heart, spirit. Not just neurons firing. All of you responding to the One who made you.

If Jesus says do not be anxious, believe that. Trust that. Not as a nice idea. As truth that can change your mind, regulate your body, and guard your soul.

This changed everything for me. And it can change everything for you.
When the constraints feel like threats, go back to this verse. Speak it. Sing it. Pray it. Let it guard your heart. Let it guard your mind.

You have to get it into your mind. Memorization. Music. Repetition. Not just reading it once. Living it. Vocalizing it. Throwing yourself into it. Letting it rewire you. Mind, body, soul.

You do not have to carry the anxiety. You were never meant to.

# FROM FREEZE TO FLIGHT: HOW GOD ACTIVATES OUR DESIGN

Fight or flight. Your nervous system responding to the question we talked about earlier. Is action required right now? Or can it wait?

When the answer is now, your body mobilizes. Fight or flight. When the answer is wait, you freeze.

But here is what no one tells you. Both fight and flight can be right. Sometimes you need to fight. Sometimes you need to flee. And your body knows the difference before your mind does.

The question is not whether you should fight or flight. The question is what makes your nervous system say now instead of wait. What flips that switch for you is different from what flips it for someone else.

God made us different. Not slightly different. Wildly, intentionally different. And He knows what activates each of us. What moves you from freeze to action is not the same as what moves someone else. And trying to force yourself to respond like they do will keep you stuck.

Here is what I have seen. There are four general patterns. You might be one of them. You might be a mix. But somewhere in here, you will recognize yourself. And once you see it, you will stop fighting how you are made and start working with it.

Some people only move when there is something to win or lose. Real stakes. Urgency. A challenge in front of them. When nothing matters, they freeze. When everything is on the line, they come alive. Deadlines do not stress them. Deadlines wake them up. Pressure does not crush them. It focuses them. They are not procrastinators. They are mobilizers. Their nervous system does not respond until the outcome is real. Until then, they wait. Not because they are lazy. Because their body is conserving energy for when it actually matters.

Winston Churchill was this. Britain was facing Nazi invasion. The nation was on the line. Everyone else was paralyzed. But Churchill? The stakes activated him. "We shall never surrender." The existential threat did not crush him. It mobilized him. He did not move until everything mattered. And when it did, he became unstoppable.

God brings people like this constraints that involve risk. Challenge. Competition. Situations where they cannot coast. Where they have to show up or lose. And when they stop resisting the pressure and lean into it, they do not just survive. They thrive.

Others only move when someone else is involved. When they are alone, they freeze. When someone is counting on them, they engage. Responsibility to another person flips the switch. It is not that they need approval. It is that relational energy gives their effort direction. Working in isolation drains them. Working with people or for people activates them. Their nervous system mobilizes when connection is present. When it is not, they stall.

Esther was this. She was queen, but she was frozen. Going to the king uninvited could mean death. She did not move. Until Mordecai said, "Who knows whether you have come to the kingdom for such a time as this?" The people needed her. That activated her. "If I perish, I perish." The moment someone was counting on her, she moved.

Martin Luther King Jr. was the same. Rosa Parks was arrested. The community needed someone to lead the boycott. People were counting on him. That relational pull activated him. Not into one moment. Into an entire movement. He did not move alone. He moved because people needed him to.

God brings people like this constraints that involve others. Responsibility. Collaboration. Situations where someone else is waiting. Where they cannot disappear without letting someone down. And when they stop resisting the weight of that and embrace it, they do not feel burdened. They feel alive.

Some people only move when there is stability to maintain. When chaos surrounds them, they freeze. When someone needs them to be steady, they engage. Being the anchor flips the switch. Their nervous system mobilizes when they are needed to hold something or someone together. When that role is not clear, they drift. Commitment does not feel heavy to them. It feels clarifying. Responsibility does not drain them. It directs them.

Joseph was this. Sold into slavery. Falsely accused. Thrown into prison. Everywhere he went, chaos surrounded him. But Joseph did not crumble. He became the one holding things together. In Potiphar's house, he ran everything. In prison, he managed it. When Pharaoh needed someone steady to save Egypt from famine, Joseph was activated. Not because the situation was easy. Because someone needed him to be the anchor. That is what moved him. That is what always moved him.

God brings people like this constraints that involve dependability. Long term commitment. Situations where they are the one people lean on. Where their consistency matters. And when they stop resisting the weight of being needed and accept it, they do not feel trapped. They feel grounded.

Others only move when there is a clear path. When everything is ambiguous, they freeze. When the steps are defined, they engage. Structure flips the switch. Their nervous system mobilizes when there is a process to follow. When the variables are too many or the expectations are unclear, they shut down. Clarity does not restrict them. It releases them. Systems do not box them in. They organize them.

God brings people like this constraints that involve order. Clear frameworks. Defined expectations. Situations where they know exactly what right looks like. And when they stop resisting the structure and step into it, they do not feel confined. They feel capable.

You are one of these. Maybe a combination. But you are not all of them. And that is the point.

What flips the switch for you is not what flips it for someone else. And God knows that. He is not confused about how you are wired. He made you that way.

Sometimes God brings the constraint directly. A call. A responsibility. A situation you did not choose but cannot ignore. Sometimes this broken world brings it. A crisis. A loss. A pressure you did not ask for. Either way, your body knows when to move. And it knows when to stay still.

The problem is not that you are frozen. The problem is that you are waiting for the wrong signal. You are waiting for motivation when your body is waiting for constraint. You are waiting for inspiration when your body is waiting for pressure. You are waiting for clarity when your body is waiting for urgency.

Once you recognize what actually moves you, everything changes. You stop trying to force yourself to respond like someone else. You stop beating yourself up for not engaging when there is no signal your body recognizes. You start paying attention to the constraints already in your life. The ones you have been fighting. The ones you thought were in your way.

And you realize they are not blocking you. They are activating you.

God knows how you are designed. He knows what moves you from freeze to action. And He is not withholding that from you. He is placing it in your life. Not to crush you. To wake you up.

The constraint is not the enemy. Resisting it is.

When you stop fighting how you are made and start recognizing the signal your body is waiting for, you do not just survive. You move. You finish. You build.

Not because you finally figured out how to be disciplined. But because you finally understood how you were designed.

If you want to go deeper into understanding which type you are and how that reflects God's image in you, that's what my book Remarkably Made explores. But for now, know this: you are designed on purpose, and the constraints in your life are not accidents.

# WHEN FLIGHT IS RIGHT

Not all constraints are from God. But God is sovereign over all things. He allows what He does not cause. And sometimes He brings crushing that refines you.

There is crushing that forms. And crushing that destroys. Your body knows the difference.

God does crush. Isaiah 48 verse 10. "Behold, I have refined you, but not as silver; I have tried you in the furnace of affliction."

The furnace of affliction. That is real. That is God's work. And it is painful.

But even in that crushing, there is purpose. There is refining. There is growth. You are being formed into something stronger, purer, more complete.

Crushing that destroys is different. It has no purpose but harm. It does not refine. It breaks. It isolates. It convinces you that you are nothing. And God does not do that.

So here is how you know the difference.

Sometimes your body goes into flight. And that is not weakness. That is wisdom.

There is a difference between God's yoke and bondage. Jesus said it Himself. Matthew 11 verse 28 through 30. "Come to me, all who labor and are heavy laden, and I will give you rest. Take my yoke upon you, and learn from me, for I am gentle and lowly in heart, and you will find rest for your souls. For my yoke is easy, and my burden is light."

Easy. Light. That is His yoke.

If the constraint you are under is crushing you without purpose, controlling you, breaking you down with no refining, that is not His yoke. That is bondage. And Galatians 5 verse 1 is clear. "For freedom Christ has set us free; stand firm therefore, and do not submit again to a yoke of slavery." Do not submit again to a yoke of slavery.

Your nervous system going into flight mode might not be fear. It might be God saying get out.

This is important. Because everything I have said in this book about welcoming constraints can be twisted. It can be used to keep you in situations that are destroying you. And I will not let that happen.

God's constraints form you. Abusive constraints deform you. God's constraints press you but do not break you. They are hard, but they produce steadfastness, maturity, completion. James 1 verse 2 through 4. The testing of your faith produces steadfastness. And steadfastness has its full effect, that you may be perfect and complete, lacking in nothing.

Perfect and complete. Not shattered and empty.

Abusive constraints do the opposite. They tear you down. They make you smaller. They isolate you. They convince you that you are nothing without them. They demand more and more and give nothing back. They do not produce steadfastness. They produce trauma.

God's constraints come with His presence. Even in the hardest seasons, He is there. You feel held. You feel seen. You may be pressed, but you are not abandoned. 2 Corinthians 4 verse 8 through 9. "We are afflicted in every way, but not crushed; perplexed, but not driven to despair; persecuted, but not forsaken; struck down, but not destroyed."

Not crushed. Not driven to despair. Not forsaken. Not destroyed.

If you are being crushed without purpose, driven to despair with no hope, forsaken with no presence, destroyed with no refining, that is not God's hand. That is something else.

Abusive constraints isolate you from God. They tell you that you are alone. That no one will understand. That no one will believe you. That you deserve this. That God has abandoned you. That is a lie. And your body knows it is a lie even when your mind believes it.

God's constraints do not require you to lose yourself. They refine you, but they do not erase you. You are still you. Your voice still matters. Your boundaries still matter. You are not required to disappear in order to be faithful.

Abusive constraints demand that you disappear. That you silence yourself. That you have no needs, no voice, no boundaries. That everything you are exists only to serve someone else's control. That is not submission. That is erasure.

Scripture is full of moments where God tells His people to flee.

Genesis 19 verse 17. The angels tell Lot, "Escape for your life. Do not look back or stop anywhere in the valley. Escape to the hills, lest you be swept away."

Flee. Do not look back. Your life depends on it.

Matthew 10 verse 23. Jesus tells His disciples, "When they persecute you in one town, flee to the next."

Flee. Do not stay and endure abuse in the name of faithfulness. Flee.

1 Corinthians 6 verse 18. "Flee from sexual immorality."
Not resist it. Not endure it. Flee from it.

Your body knows when to run. And sometimes running is the most faithful thing you can do.

If you are in a relationship where someone controls you, isolates you, demeans you, harms you, that is not a constraint from God. That is abuse. And you are not required to stay.
If you are in a job that is destroying your health, your family, your soul, and there is no light, no growth, no hope, just grinding you down, that is not a God given constraint. That is exploitation. And you are not required to endure it in the name of perseverance.

If you are in a church or community that manipulates you, shames you, controls you, silences you, weaponizes Scripture against you, that is not godly accountability. That is spiritual abuse. And you are not required to submit to it.

Flight is not always fear. Sometimes it is obedience.

Your nervous system is not lying to you when it screams run. Sometimes God is the one telling you to move.

Do not let anyone use this book to keep you in bondage. Do not let anyone tell you that welcoming constraints means accepting abuse. It does not.

There is a yoke that is easy and a burden that is light. And there is a yoke of slavery. Learn the difference. And when you recognize slavery, flee.

God does not call you to be destroyed. He calls you to be held. And if the constraint you are under is crushing you without refining you, destroying you without forming you, it is not from Him.

Trust your body. Trust the One who made it. And when He says run, run.

"Escape for your life. Do not look back or stop anywhere in the valley. Escape to the hills, lest you be swept away." Genesis 19:17

# THE SHIFT: WHAT CHANGES WHEN YOU STOP RESISTING

Something shifts when you stop fighting.

It is not dramatic. It is not a lightning bolt moment where everything suddenly makes sense and you never struggle again. It is quieter than that. But it is real.

You wake up and the constraint is still there. The deadline. The responsibility. The pressure. But it does not feel the same. It does not feel like a threat. It feels like a signal.

Your body knows what to do with it now.

That is the first thing that changes. Your body stops fighting itself.

For years, you have been at war with yourself. Trying to force yourself to move when there was no signal your nervous system recognized. Beating yourself up for not being disciplined. Wondering what was wrong with you. Why everyone else could just do the thing and you could not.

Now you know. Nothing is wrong with you. You were waiting for the wrong signal.

And once you stop waiting for motivation and start recognizing constraint, your body relaxes. Not because the pressure is gone. Because the pressure finally makes sense. You stop feeling anxious about not starting. You stop lying in bed wondering why you cannot move. You stop circling ideas that never land. Because now you know. You are not lazy. You are not broken. You are uncontained. And the constraint you were fighting is the very thing that helps you engage.

That shift changes how you move through your day.

You stop resenting the deadline. You lean into it. You stop avoiding the responsibility. You accept it. You stop trying to clear the field before you start. You work under the constraint. In the gaps. In the pressure. And you finish things.

Not because you suddenly became someone else. Because you finally stopped fighting who you are.

Your work changes. You stop starting projects you never finish. You stop having a thousand ideas that go nowhere. You stop thinking that someday when you have more time, you will finally do the thing. You realize the time is now. The constraint is here. And that is not a problem. That is the condition you need.

You write the book in two days because the deadline is real. You finish the project because someone is counting on you. You show up because the responsibility is clear. You do not wait for perfect conditions. You work with what is in front of you.

And it works. Not perfectly. But it works.

Your relationships change too. You stop pretending you can show up for everyone all the time. You stop carrying what is not yours to carry. You recognize when you are the one who needs to be steady and when you need to step back. You stop apologizing for needing pressure to move. You stop pretending you work like everyone else.

You let people see how you actually function. And the ones who matter do not judge you for it. They adjust. They give you the constraint you need. They stop offering you wide open space and start giving you clear deadlines or real responsibility or defined structure. And you thrive under it.
The people who do not understand? You stop trying to explain it to them. You stop trying to be what they think you should be. You accept that God made you different. And that is not something to apologize for.

You also stop feeling guilty for needing what you need. You stop thinking that needing a deadline makes you a procrastinator. You stop thinking that needing someone to count on you makes you dependent. You stop thinking that needing structure makes you rigid. You stop thinking that needing stakes makes you adrenaline addicted.

You recognize that these are not flaws. These are how you are designed. And God does not make mistakes.

Your relationship with God changes too. You stop thinking He is disappointed in you for not being more disciplined. You stop praying for Him to give you motivation. You stop asking Him to remove the constraints.

You start thanking Him for them. You start recognizing that the deployment, the certifications, the responsibilities, the pressure, all of it, was Him placing exactly what you needed in your life. Not to punish you. To activate you.

You stop seeing Him as the one holding you back. You start seeing Him as the one holding you together.

And when the crushing comes, because it will come, you do not spiral the same way. You ask different questions. Is this refining me or destroying me? Is this God's yoke or bondage? Is this forming me or deforming me? And you trust your body to know the difference.

When it is refining, you stay. You lean in. You let the constraint press you into something stronger. When it is destroying, you flee. And you do not apologize for it.

That is the shift. You stop second guessing yourself. You stop wondering if you are doing it right. You start trusting that

God made you on purpose. And the constraints in your life are not accidents.

But here is what does not change. You still struggle. You still have days where you do not want to move. You still resist sometimes. You still wish things were easier.

This is not a one-time revelation that fixes everything forever. This is an ongoing practice. Every day, you wake up and choose. Do I fight the constraint or do I welcome it? Do I resist how I am made or do I work with it?

Some days you choose well. Some days you do not. And that is okay. Because you are not trying to be perfect. You are trying to be obedient. And obedience looks like recognizing the constraint, accepting it, and moving under it.

It looks like finishing the thing even when it is hard. It looks like showing up even when you do not feel like it. It looks like trusting that God knows what He is doing even when you do not understand.

And over time, the shift becomes more natural. You stop defaulting to resistance. You start defaulting to recognition. You see the constraint and instead of thinking this is in my way, you think this is the way.

That does not mean it stops being hard. It just means you stop being surprised that it is hard. You stop thinking something is wrong because it requires effort. You accept that effort is part of the design.

You also stop comparing yourself to other people. You stop wondering why they can work in open space and you cannot. You stop thinking you should be like them. You recognize that they are wired differently. And that is fine. Their design is not better than yours. It is just different.

You start celebrating how you are made instead of apologizing for it. You start recognizing the constraints that work for you instead of forcing yourself into the ones that do not. You start finishing things. Not because you became disciplined. But because you stopped resisting the very thing that makes finishing possible.

The shift is not perfection. It is clarity. You stop asking what is wrong with me. You start asking what does my body need to move. And you trust that God has already provided it. The constraint is here. It is not going away. And you do not need it to.

Because now you know. The constraint is not the enemy. It is the gift. And you are finally ready to stop fighting it.

# NOW YOU MOVE

You know now.

You know your nervous system needs constraints to move. You know God designed limits before anything broke. You know the constraints in your life are not accidents. You know how you are wired. You know when to fight and when to flee. So what now?

Now you live held.

Not by your performance. Not by your ability to finally get it together. Not by whether you finish everything or accomplish what you said you would.

You live held by God. By the One who knows how you are made. Who set the boundaries that hold creation together. Who brings the constraints you need. Who stays with you in the furnace. Who tells you when to run.

Living held does not mean the constraints go away. It means you stop resisting them.

You stop waiting for life to clear. You stop thinking that freedom means no limits. You stop fighting the very thing that would help you move.

You welcome the constraint.

Not because it feels good. But because you trust the One who placed it.

This is not passive. This is not giving up. This is not settling for less than you were meant for.

This is recognizing that the constraint is not blocking your calling. It is the condition under which your calling becomes real.

Living held looks like this.

You stop apologizing for how you are wired. You stop trying to be someone else. You stop forcing yourself to respond to signals your body does not recognize. You pay attention to what actually moves you. And you stop calling that a flaw.

You recognize the constraints already in your life. The ones you have been fighting. The deadline. The responsibility. The structure. The challenge. And instead of resenting them, you lean into them. You let them do what they were designed to do. Activate you. Focus you. Move you.

You stop manufacturing pressure that does not work. You stop building systems that someone else swears by but leave you frozen. You stop pretending you can engineer your way into discipline. You accept that God brings what you need. Not what you want. And you trust that He knows the difference.

You stop waiting for the perfect conditions. You stop thinking that someday when things settle down, when you have more time, when the pressure lifts, then you will finally do what matters. You realize that the pressure is not in your way. It is the way.

You work under the constraint. In the gaps. In the tight windows. With the deadlines. With the people counting on you. With the structure. With the stakes. You stop treating those as obstacles and start treating them as the very thing making it possible.

You finish things. Not because you suddenly became disciplined. But because you stopped fighting yourself.

Living held also means you let go of what is not yours to carry.

You are not responsible for holding everyone together. You are not required to fix what God has not asked you to fix. You are not obligated to stay in situations that destroy you in the name of faithfulness.

You trust that God is sovereign. That He allows what He does not cause. That He refines through crushing but does not destroy through it. And when the crushing has no purpose but harm, you flee. You do not apologize for it. You obey.

Living held means you stop proving yourself. You stop striving to earn what you already have. You are complete in Christ. Colossians 2 verse 10. You have been filled in Him. You do not need to become more to be enough. You already are.

The constraint is not there to prove you are capable. It is there to show you that you are held.

Even when you fail. Even when you do not finish. Even when the constraint crushes you and you cry out and wonder where God is. You are held.

That does not change based on your performance. That does not shift based on whether you got it right. You are held because He holds you. Not because you hold yourself together.

This changes how you see everything.

The deployment is not a threat. It is the condition under which you write the book. The certifications are not in your way. They are the pressure that makes you move. The responsibilities are not too much. They are what your body recognizes as now.

The constraints are not the enemy. They are the design.

And you do not have to carry them alone.

Psalm 55 verse 22. "Cast your burden on the LORD, and he will sustain you; he will never permit the righteous to be moved."

Cast your burden. Not carry it in your own strength. Not pretend it is not heavy. Cast it. Give it to Him. And He will sustain you.

That is what living held looks like. You carry what He gives you to carry. You welcome the constraint He places. And you trust that He is sustaining you through it.

This is not easy. No one said it would be easy. Jesus said His yoke is easy and His burden is light. But He did not say there would be no yoke. He did not say there would be no burden. He said take mine.

Living held means you take His yoke. Not the one you build. Not the one someone else built. Not the one this world tries to put on you. His.

And His yoke fits. It is designed for you. It does not crush you. It carries you.

So what now?

Now you stop waiting. You stop resisting. You stop pretending that freedom means no limits.

You welcome the constraint. You recognize the signal your body is waiting for. You lean into the pressure. You work under the conditions God has placed in your life. And you trust that He knows what He is doing.

You are not broken. You are held.

The constraints are not going away. And that is good news.
Because the constraint is not the problem. It never was.
The constraint is the gift. And you are finally ready to receive it.

# EPILOGUE
*Start Small. Stay Held.*

If this book did its job, you are not inspired right now. You are steadier.

You may also feel an unfamiliar urge to do less, not more. To stop chasing a version of freedom that never quite delivered and instead begin paying attention to what actually holds you together.

That is the right instinct.

The mistake many people make at this point is trying to overhaul their entire .life. New systems. New rules. New commitments. That impulse comes from the same place as the old one. Too much space. Too many options. Too little containment.

This is not a call to redesign everything. It is an invitation to notice one thing.

Where does your life already hold together?

There is almost always a place where you show up consistently. A role you do not abandon. A responsibility you do not negotiate with yourself about. A constraint that quietly works. Start there. That is not coincidence. That is information.

You do not need to add pressure everywhere. You need to recognize where pressure already produces clarity and allow that pattern to guide you.

Pay attention to the constraint already in your life. The one you have been fighting. The deadline. The responsibility. The structure. The challenge. Stop resisting it. Welcome it. Let it do what it was designed to do.

You do not need to prove anything to yourself. You do not need to catch up. You do not need to justify why this has been hard.

You are not broken. You were uncontained.

Start with one boundary that brings relief instead of resistance. Let it hold. Let it become familiar. Let direction emerge before ambition returns.

This is how things that last are built. Quietly. Deliberately. Within limits that care enough to keep you intact.

And remember this. You are held. Not by your ability to get it together. Not by your performance. Not by whether you finish everything you start.

You are held by God. By the One who set the stars in place and knows your name. By the One who brings the constraint and sustains you through it. By the One whose yoke is easy and whose burden is light.

That does not change based on how well you do today. That does not shift based on whether you got it right. You are held because He holds you.

So start small. Pay attention. Welcome the constraint. And trust that He knows what He is doing.

The constraint is not going away. And that is good news.

Now you move.

www.ingramcontent.com/pod-product-compliance
Lightning Source LLC
Chambersburg PA
CBHW031633040426

42452CB00007B/802